Key Stage 2

Number Patterns & Algebra

Hilary Koll and Steve Mills

Name _____

Schofield & Sims

Introduction

Recognising and understanding patterns is an important skill in mathematics, and one which can be used in many ways. In this book you will learn how to recognise, extend and explain number sequences, using and applying known number facts. You will also learn some simple algebra which can be used to explain some of the patterns you find.

How to use this book

Before you start using this book, write your name in the name box on the first page.

Then decide how to begin. If you want a complete course on number patterns and simple algebra, you should work right through the book from beginning to end. Another way to use the book is to dip into it when you want to find out about a particular topic, such as fraction sequences. The Contents page will help you to find the pages you need.

Whichever way you choose, don't try to do too much at once – it's better to work through the book in short bursts.

When you have found the topic you want to study, look out for these icons, which mark different parts of the text.

This icon shows you the activities that you should complete. You write your answers in the spaces provided. You might find it useful to have some spare paper to work on for some of the activities. After you have worked through all the activities on the page, turn to pages 45–49 at the end of the book to check your answers. When you are sure that you understand the topic, put a tick in the box beside it on the Contents page.

On pages 10, 21, 28 and 34 you will find **Progress tests**. These contain questions that will check your understanding of the topics that you have worked through so far. Check your answers on page 50. It is important that you correct any mistakes before moving on to the next section.

On pages 41–44 you will find a **Final test**. This will check your understanding of all the topics. Check your answers on page 51.

Explanation

This text explains the topic and gives examples. Make sure you read it before you start the activities.

This text gives you useful background information about the subject.

Contents

Odd and even numbers

Explanation

Every whole number is either **even** or **odd**.

Even numbers are whole numbers that can be divided exactly by **2** to give a whole number.

Example **24 ÷ 2 = 12**   so **24** is an **even** number.

All numbers that end in **0**, **2**, **4**, **6** and **8** are **even** numbers.

Example **6**   **18**   **54**   **270**   **832**

Odd numbers are whole numbers that cannot be divided exactly by **2** to give a whole number.

Example **25 ÷ 2 = 12** r **1**   so **25** is an **odd** number.

All numbers that end in **1**, **3**, **5**, **7** and **9** are **odd** numbers.

Example **3**   **15**   **67**   **121**   **659**

Activities

1   Draw a ring around any **even** numbers you can see in this list.

23   **56**   **78**   **109**   **814**   **157**

2   Draw a ring around any **odd** numbers you can see in this list.

28   **52**   **99**   **175**   **426**   **681**

3   Give some examples to match these statements.

a   The numbers on both sides of an odd number are even.

6, 7, 8

b   The sum of three odd numbers is odd.

c   The difference between any two even numbers or any two odd numbers is even.

d   When two even numbers are multiplied the answer is even.

Counting on from zero in steps of 2, 5, 3, 4 and 8

Explanation

A number sequence is a list of numbers arranged in a particular order and according to a rule.

Example

2, 4, 6, 8, 10 . . .
add **2**

1, 3, 9, 27, 81 . . .
multiply by **3**

Look for patterns in the numbers when continuing sequences.

- Counting on in equal steps of **2** from zero produces even numbers.
- Counting on in equal steps of **5** from zero produces numbers ending in **0** or **5**.
- Counting on in equal steps of **3** from zero produces alternate odd and even numbers.
- Counting on in equal steps of **4** from zero produces even numbers.
- Counting on in equal steps of **8** from zero produces even numbers.

Activities

1 Count on to continue these sequences:

a in twos   0, 2, ____ ____ ____ ____ ____ ____ ____ ____ ____

b in fives   0, 5, ____ ____ ____ ____ ____ ____ ____ ____ ____

c in threes   0, 3, ____ ____ ____ ____ ____ ____ ____ ____ ____

d in fours   0, 4, ____ ____ ____ ____ ____ ____ ____ ____ ____

e in eights   0, 8, ____ ____ ____ ____ ____ ____ ____ ____ ____

2 Compare numbers in pairs of sequences.

a Compare counting in twos and fours. What do you notice?

_____

b Compare counting in fours and eights. What do you notice?

_____

3 Fill in the missing numbers in these sequences.

a 72, 56, 48, 40, ____ , 24, ____ , 8, ____

b 33, 30, ____ , 24, ____ , 18, 15, ____ , 9, 6, 3

c 48, ____ , 40, ____ , 32, ____ , 24, 20, 16, ____ , 8

Counting on and back in tens

Explanation

Counting on and back in tens is easy because the unit digit stays the same.

Sequences don't always have to start with zero. You can count on or back starting with any number.

Counting on in tens from 5

5   15   25   35   45   55   65   75   85   95   105 ...

Counting back in tens from 127

127   117   107   97   87   77   67   57   47   37   27 ...

Activities

1   Count on in tens starting from:

    a   60 _____

    b   93 _____

2   Count back in tens starting from:

    a   152 _____

    b   218 _____

3   Fill in the missing numbers in these sequences.

  a | ☐ | ☐ | 57 | 67 | 77 | ☐ | ☐ | ☐ | ☐ | ☐ |

  b | ☐ | ☐ | ☐ | ☐ | ☐ | 123 | 133 | 143 | ☐ | ☐ |

  c | ☐ | ☐ | ☐ | 175 | ☐ | ☐ | ☐ | 135 | ☐ | ☐ |

  d | ☐ | ☐ | 368 | ☐ | ☐ | ☐ | 328 | ☐ | ☐ | ☐ |

  e | 6216 | 6226 | ☐ | ☐ | 6256 | ☐ | ☐ | ☐ | ☐ | ☐ |

  f | ☐ | 1184 | ☐ | ☐ | ☐ | 1214 | ☐ | 1234 | ☐ | ☐ |

Counting on and back in hundreds

Explanation

Counting on and back in hundreds is also easy because all the tens and unit digits stay the same.

Counting on in hundreds

5   105   205   305   405   505   605   705   805   905   1005 ...

Counting back in hundreds

1426   1326   1226   1126   1026   926   826   726 ...

Activities

1   Count on in hundreds starting from:

a   300   _____

b   853   _____

c   1542   _____

2   Count back in hundreds starting from:

a   1400   _____

b   3782   _____

c   7861   _____

3   Fill in the missing numbers in these sequences.

a

	1100	1200			1500				

b

				6617			6917		

c

	5342				4942				

d

			7551					7051	

e

			8736	8836					

Recognising multiples of 2, 3, 4, 5 and 10

Explanation

A **multiple** is a number that is in a times table or beyond.

Multiples are created when counting on in equal steps from zero.

Example multiples of **4** are **4**, **8**, **12**, **16**, **20**, **24**, **28**, **32** ... and they carry on in fours.

Example multiples of **10** go up in tens and include **50**, **60**, **230** and **1690**.

Activities

1 Write any five multiples of:

a 2 ____ ____ ____ ____ ____   b 3 ____ ____ ____ ____ ____

c 5 ____ ____ ____ ____ ____   d 8 ____ ____ ____ ____ ____

e 50 ____ ____ ____ ____ ____   f 100 ____ ____ ____ ____ ____

2 Draw a ring around the numbers that are:

a

multiples of **2**

15   44   7

41   9   12

6   60   27

100   38   94

b

multiples of **3**

25   37   9

42   18   12

15   40   27

63   39   91

c

multiples of **4**

15   44   7

41   9   12

6   60   27

100   38   94

d

multiples of **5**

25   37   9

42   18   12

15   40   27

63   39   91

3 Use the key to draw the correct shapes around the numbers.

Key	
☐	multiples of **3**
△	multiples of **4**
◯	multiples of **10**

50   36   40

100   160   30

△12△   32   56   84   120

Number Patterns & Algebra

Counting in multiples of 25, 50, 100, 250 and 1000

When continuing sequences of multiples of **50**, remember that two lots of **50** is **100**, so every other number will be a multiple of **100**.

When continuing sequences of multiples of **25**, remember that four lots of **25** is **100**, so every fourth number will be a multiple of **100**.

Activities

1 Count on in fifties to continue the sequences.

   a 450 _____ _____ _____ _____ _____ _____

   b 1250 _____ _____ _____ _____ _____ _____

   c 8800 _____ _____ _____ _____ _____ _____

2 Count on in twenty-fives to continue the sequences.

   a 325 _____ _____ _____ _____ _____ _____

   b 3550 _____ _____ _____ _____ _____ _____

   c 7875 _____ _____ _____ _____ _____ _____

3 Continue each sequence and then circle all the numbers that appear in more than one row.

   a Add **25**

6025	6050	6075							

   b Add **500**

3500	4000	4500							

   c Add _____

7350	7400	7450							

   d Add _____

4000	5000	6000							

   e Add _____

6750	7000	7250							

Progress test 1

1 Count on in threes from zero.

0 _____ _____ _____ _____ _____ _____ _____ _____ _____ _____

2 Count on in eights from zero.

0 _____ _____ _____ _____ _____ _____ _____ _____ _____ _____

3 Count on in tens starting from:

78 _____ _____ _____ _____ _____ _____ _____ _____ _____

4 Fill in the missing numbers in this sequence.

☐ — ☐ — ☐ — ☐ — ☐ — 116 — 106 — 96 — ☐ — ☐

5 Count on in hundreds starting from:

294 _____ _____ _____ _____ _____ _____ _____ _____ _____

6 Count back in hundreds starting from:

3672 _____ _____ _____ _____ _____ _____ _____ _____

7 Draw a ring around any **even** numbers you can see in this list.

34   67   182   780   1653   2889

8 Write any five multiples of:

a 3 _____ _____ _____ _____ _____   **b** 4 _____ _____ _____ _____ _____

9 Use the key to draw the correct shapes around the numbers.

4325   675   350

1200   1250   8400

4630   1720   3075

Key	
☐	multiples of 25
○	multiples of 50
△	multiples of 100

Counting on from zero in steps of 6, 7 and 9

Activities

1 Count on to continue these sequences:

    a in sixes   0, 6, _____

    b in sevens   0, 7, _____

    c in nines   0, 9, _____

2 What do you notice about all the numbers in the sequence of sixes?

_____

3 Which numbers appear in:

    a both the sequence of sixes and the sequence of sevens?   _____

    b both the sequence of sevens and the sequence of nines?   _____

    c both the sequence of sixes and the sequence of nines?   _____

4 This is the sequence of threes: **0, 3, 6, 9, 12, 15, 18, 21, 24, 27, 30, 33, 36 ...**

    a Compare counting in threes and sixes. What do you notice?

_____

    b Compare counting in threes and nines. What do you notice?

_____

5 Fill in the missing numbers in these sequences.

    a 84, 77, 70, _____, 56, _____, 42, _____, _____, 21 ...

    b 36, _____, 48, _____, 60, _____, _____, 78 ...

    c 99, 90, _____, 72, _____, 54, 45, _____, 27, 18, 9 ...

    d 72, _____, _____, 54, _____, 42, _____, 30, 24 ...

Recognising multiples of 6, 7, 8 and 9

Activities

1 Write any five multiples of:

   a 6 ____ ____ ____ ____ ____   **b** 7 ____ ____ ____ ____ ____

   c 8 ____ ____ ____ ____ ____   **d** 9 ____ ____ ____ ____ ____

2 Draw a ring around the numbers that are:

a
> multiples of **6**
>
> 18   44   52
> 48   26   60
> 6   90   27
> 100   38   84

b
> multiples of **7**
>
> 27   37   35
> 42   53   63
> 56   40   29
> 70   107   105

c
> multiples of **8**
>
> 34   40   72
> 46   58   16
> 24   50   100
> 88   38   92

d
> multiples of **9**
>
> 27   39   90
> 46   54   72
> 45   41   99
> 63   36   91

3 Use the key to draw the correct shapes around the numbers.

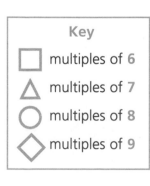

Key

☐ multiples of **6**

△ multiples of **7**

◯ multiples of **8**

◇ multiples of **9**

48   100   36   40   16   35

120   72   56   84   42

63   90   98

60   45   78   96   168

Finding missing numbers in sequences

Explanation

Sometimes you are asked to fill in the gaps in sequences where you don't know the steps you are counting in, like this:

Example Fill in the missing numbers in this sequence.   6 ____ ____ ____ ____ 21

To help you solve this, first look at this sequence.

4   6   8   10   12   14
    2   2   2   2   2

Imagine you had been given just the first and last numbers.

4 ____ ____ ____ ____ **14**

The difference between **4** and **14** is **10**. Count the **gaps** (**not** the missing numbers) between **4** and **14**. There are **five** gaps.

Divide the difference by the number of gaps.

10 ÷ 5 = 2 so each number is **2** more than the one before it.

Now use this method for the example question above.

6 ____ ____ ____ ____ **21**

The difference between **6** and **21** is **15**. There are **five** gaps (don't count the **four** missing numbers).

15 ÷ 5 = 3 so each number is **3** more than the one before it.

6   9   12   15   18   21

Activities

1 Fill in the missing numbers in these sequences.

    a 9 ____ ____ ____ ____ 29   **b** 12 ____ ____ ____ ____ 37

    c 17 ____ ____ ____ ____ 47   **d** 19 ____ ____ ____ ____ 54

    e 154 ____ ____ ____ ____ 99   **f** 207 ____ ____ ____ ____ 147

2 Fill in the missing numbers in these sequences.

    a [ ] [ ] [45] [ ] [ ] [ ] [57] [ ] [ ]

    b [ ] [73] [ ] [ ] [ ] [ ] [38] [ ]

    c [ ] [ ] [ ] [101] [ ] [ ] [ ] [185]

Explaining number sequences

Explanation

If you are asked to continue a number sequence and then to explain it, begin by looking at the **difference** between the numbers. Write a 'line of differences', using words like 'difference', 'larger', 'smaller', 'decreasing' and 'increasing'.

Example

1. Explain this pattern.   6   15   24   33   42   ...

   line of differences ⟶   9   9   9   9

   The numbers in this sequence start at **6** and get larger by a difference of **9** each time.

2. Explain this pattern.   7   8   10   13   17   ...

   line of differences ⟶   1   2   3   4

   This sequence starts at **7** and the difference between each number increases by **1** each time.

Activities

1   Continue each sequence and then explain it.

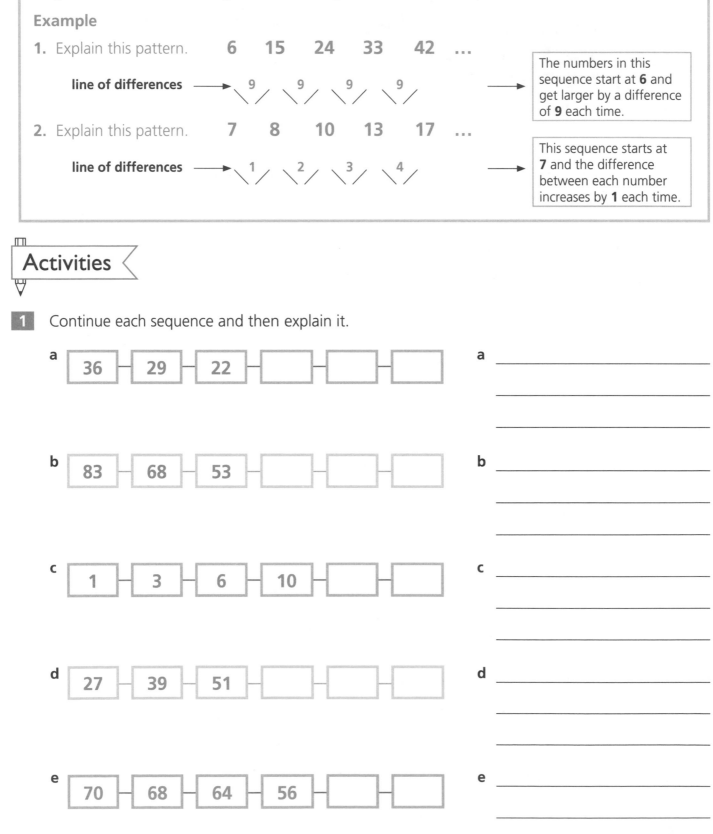

a   36   29   22   ☐   ☐   ☐

a _____
_____
_____

b   83   68   53   ☐   ☐   ☐

b _____
_____
_____

c   1   3   6   10   ☐   ☐

c _____
_____
_____

d   27   39   51   ☐   ☐   ☐

d _____
_____
_____

e   70   68   64   56   ☐   ☐

e _____
_____
_____

Fraction sequences

Explanation

You can count on or back in whole numbers to create sequences but you can also count in smaller steps, such as in halves or quarters.

If counting in multiples of $\frac{1}{2}$ every other number will be a whole number.

If counting in multiples of $\frac{1}{4}$ every fourth number will be a whole number.

If counting in multiples of $\frac{1}{3}$ every third number will be a whole number.

Activities

1 Count on or back in steps of $\frac{1}{2}$ to continue the sequences.

   a $2\frac{1}{2}$ 3 $3\frac{1}{2}$ 4   ___   ___   ___   ___   ___

   b $12\frac{1}{2}$ 12 $11\frac{1}{2}$ 11   ___   ___   ___   ___

2 Count on or back in steps of $\frac{1}{4}$ to continue the sequences.

   a $4\frac{1}{2}$ $4\frac{3}{4}$ 5 $5\frac{1}{4}$ ___   ___   ___   ___   ___

   b $19\frac{1}{4}$ 19 $18\frac{3}{4}$ $18\frac{1}{2}$ ___   ___   ___   ___   ___

3 Count on or back in steps of $\frac{1}{3}$ to continue the sequences.

   a 3 $3\frac{1}{3}$ $3\frac{2}{3}$ 4   ___   ___   ___   ___   ___

   b $16\frac{1}{3}$ 16 $15\frac{2}{3}$ $15\frac{1}{3}$ ___   ___   ___   ___

4 Continue each sequence and then explain it.

   a [8]–[$7\frac{2}{3}$]–[$7\frac{1}{3}$]–[   ]–[   ]–[   ]   **a** _____

_____

_____

   b [$4\frac{3}{4}$]–[5]–[$5\frac{1}{4}$]–[   ]–[   ]–[   ]   **b** _____

_____

_____

   c [21]–[$20\frac{1}{2}$]–[20]–[   ]–[   ]–[   ]   **c** _____

_____

_____

Tenths and hundredths

Explanation

When a whole is split into **10** equal parts each part is one-tenth. This can be written as a fraction $\frac{1}{10}$ or as a decimal **0.1**.

When a whole is split into **100** equal parts each part is one-hundredth. This can be written as a fraction $\frac{1}{100}$ or as a decimal **0.01**.

When counting with fractions, answers greater than one whole can be given as mixed numbers, such as $1\frac{1}{10}$ or as top-heavy (improper) fractions, such as $\frac{11}{10}$.

Activities

1 Count on in tenths.

a $\frac{1}{10}$, $\frac{2}{10}$, $\frac{3}{10}$, $\frac{4}{10}$, $\frac{}{10}$, $\frac{}{10}$, $\frac{7}{10}$, $\frac{}{10}$, $\frac{9}{10}$, $\frac{10}{10}$, $\frac{11}{10}$, $\frac{12}{10}$, $\frac{}{10}$, $\frac{}{10}$, $\frac{15}{10}$ ...

Circle the fractions that show one whole and one half.

b $\frac{8}{10}$, $\frac{9}{10}$, 1, $1\frac{1}{10}$, $1\frac{2}{10}$, ☐, ☐, $1\frac{5}{10}$, ☐, ☐, ☐, ☐, ☐ ...

Circle the mixed number that shows one and a half.

c 0.1, 0.2, 0.3, ____, 0.5, ____, 0.7, 0.8, ____, 1, 1.1, 1.2, ____, 1.4 ...

Circle the decimal that shows one-half.

2 Count on in hundredths.

a $\frac{1}{100}$, $\frac{2}{100}$, $\frac{3}{100}$, $\frac{4}{100}$, $\frac{}{100}$, $\frac{}{100}$, $\frac{}{100}$, $\frac{}{100}$, $\frac{}{100}$, $\frac{10}{100}$, $\frac{11}{100}$, $\frac{}{100}$, $\frac{}{100}$ ...

Circle the fraction that shows one-tenth.

b $\frac{98}{100}$, $\frac{99}{100}$, 1, $1\frac{1}{100}$, ☐, ☐, $1\frac{4}{100}$, ☐, ☐, ☐, ☐, ☐ ...

c 0.01, 0.02, 0.03, ____, 0.05, 0.06, 0.07, 0.08, ____, 0.1, 0.11, ____ ...

d 0.89, 0.9, 0.91, ____, 0.93, 0.94, 0.95, 0.96, ____, 0.98, 0.99, ____, 1.01 ...

Number Patterns & Algebra

Counting on and back with decimals

Explanation

Decimals can be put onto number lines to show where they lie.

This number line is marked in quarters and halves.

Did you know?

Decimal numbers, like fractions, are called 'part' numbers because they are not whole numbers. They lie **between** whole numbers.

For example **2.5** lies between **2** and **3**, and **5.25** lies **between 5** and **6**.

```
0      0.25     0.5     0.75      1      1.25     1.5     1.75      2
├───────┼────────┼───────┼────────┼───────┼────────┼───────┼────────┤
```

This number line is marked in fifths.

```
0     0.2    0.4    0.6    0.8     1     1.2    1.4    1.6    1.8     2     2.2
├──────┼──────┼──────┼──────┼──────┼──────┼──────┼──────┼──────┼──────┼──────┤
```

Drawing number lines can sometimes help to count on or back in decimals.

Activities

1 Complete these sequences.

a | 0.7 | 0.8 | 0.9 | | | | | | |

b | 1.6 | 1.8 | 2.0 | | | | | | |

c | 1.25 | 1.5 | 1.75 | | | | | | |

d | 0.5 | 1.0 | 1.5 | | | | | | |

2 Continue each sequence and then explain it.

a | 1.3 | 1.2 | 1.1 | | | |

a _____
   _____
   _____

b | 7 | 6.75 | 6.5 | | | |

b _____
   _____
   _____

c | 9.2 | 9.4 | 9.6 | | | |

c _____
   _____
   _____

Counting on and back beyond zero

Activities

1 Continue these sequences, counting back past zero.

a 9   8   7   6   ____ ____ ____ ____ ____ ____

b 4   3   2   1   ____ ____ ____ ____ ____ ____

c 0   −1   −2   −3   ____ ____ ____ ____ ____ ____

d −7   −8   −9   −10 ____ ____ ____ ____ ____ ____

2 Continue these sequences, counting on past zero.

a −1   0   1   2   ____ ____ ____ ____ ____ ____

b −4   −3   −2   −1   ____ ____ ____ ____ ____ ____

c −10   −9   −8   −7   ____ ____ ____ ____ ____ ____

d −15 −14 −13 −12 ____ ____ ____ ____ ____ ____

3 Fill in the gaps in these sequences.

a | 4 | 3 | | | | −1 | | |

b | | | −2 | | | | −6 | −7 |

c | −9 | −10 | | | | | −15 | |

Negative numbers

```
15
10
 5
 0
–5
–10
–15
        °C
```

Activities

1 Write the new temperature after each change.

   a It was **5**°C. The temperature fell by **7**°C. _____

   b It was **–3**°C. The temperature rose by **10**°C. _____

   c It was **–1**°C. The temperature fell by **6**°C. _____

   d It was **9**°C. The temperature rose by **5**°C. _____

   e It was **7**°C. The temperature fell by **21**°C. _____

2 Find the difference between each pair of temperatures.

   a –1°C   7°C _____   **b** 6°C   –9°C _____

   c –8°C   –3°C _____   **d** –20°C   –5°C _____

3 Put these temperatures in order, starting with the coldest.

   a –1°C 3°C –5°C –3°C 5°C _____

   b 8°C –4°C –10°C 0°C –1°C _____

   c –1.5°C 2°C 1.5°C –3°C –1°C _____

4 Continue these sequences.

   a 4, 2, 0, –2, –4, _____ _____ _____ _____ _____ _____

   b 25, 20, 15, 10, 5, _____ _____ _____ _____ _____ _____

   c 31, 26, 21, 16, 11, _____ _____ _____ _____ _____ _____

   d –61, –51, –41, –31, –21, _____ _____ _____ _____ _____ _____

   e –23, –20, –17, –14, –11, _____ _____ _____ _____ _____ _____

Predicting numbers in a sequence

When looking at sequences, you can predict whether a large number will be in the sequence if you carried it on.

This sequence produces multiples of **4**: **4, 8, 12, 16, 20, 24, 28 ...**

Example Will **401** be in this sequence or not?
It will not, as **401** is not a multiple of **4**.

This sequence produces numbers that
are one more than the multiples of **4**: **5, 9, 13, 17, 21, 25, 29 ...**

Example Will **401** be in this sequence or not?
401 will be in this sequence as it is one more than a multiple of **4**.

Look for other patterns too, like whether the numbers in the sequence are all odd, or all even or whether the unit digit is always **6** and so on.

Activities

1   Predict whether the number in the box will be in each sequence. Circle yes or no.

a 5, 10, 15, 20, 25, 30 35 ... | 500 | yes / no

b 6, 12, 18, 24, 30, 36 ... | 81 | yes / no

c 22, 27, 32, 37, 42, 47 ... | 73 | yes / no

d 48, 58, 68, 78, 88, 98 ... | 358 | yes / no

e 7, 15, 23, 31, 39, 47 ... | 87 | yes / no

f 14, 21, 28, 35, 42, 49 ... | 707 | yes / no

g 15, 26, 37, 48, 59, 70 ... | 124 | yes / no

h 26, 51, 76, 101, 126, 151 ... | 306 | yes / no

i 4, 7, 10, 13, 16, 19, 22 ... | 302 | yes / no

j 29, 59, 89, 119, 149 ... | 299 | yes / no

k 24, 36, 48, 60, 72, 84 ... | 132 | yes / no

Progress test 2

1 Count in sevens. 0, 7, ____ ____ ____ ____ ____ ____ ____ ____ ____ ____

2 Use the key to draw the correct shapes around the numbers.

48

45

56

92

108

84

110

128

60

63

Key

☐ multiples of 6

△ multiples of 7

○ multiples of 8

◇ multiples of 9

3 Continue the sequence and then explain it.

| 35 | 23 | 11 | | | |

_____

_____

_____

4 Fill in the missing numbers in this sequence.

| | | 36 | | | 60 | | |

5 Fill in the missing numbers in the sequences.

a 0, $\frac{1}{2}$, ☐ , $1\frac{1}{2}$, ☐ , ☐ , 3, ☐ , ☐ ...

b $\frac{4}{10}$, $\frac{5}{10}$, ____ , $\frac{7}{10}$, ____ , $\frac{9}{10}$, $\frac{10}{10}$, $\frac{11}{10}$, $\frac{12}{10}$, ____ , ____ , $\frac{15}{10}$ ...

c 0.93, 0.94, 0.95, 0.96, _____ , 0.98, 0.99, _____ , 1.01, 1.02, _____ ...

6 Continue these sequences.

a 5   4   3   2   ____ ____ ____ ____ ____

b −6   −7   −8   −9   ____ ____ ____ ____ ____

7 Fill in the gaps in this sequence.

| | 1 | | | −2 | | | |

8 Predict whether the number in the box is in each sequence. Circle yes or no.

a 8, 16, 24, 32, 40, 48, 56 ... | 482 | yes / no

b 6, 13, 20, 27, 34, 41, 48 ... | 699 | yes / no

Square numbers

Explanation

Square numbers are the result of multiplying a number by itself.

Example $1 \times 1 = 1$, $2 \times 2 = 4$, $8 \times 8 = 64$, $10 \times 10 = 100$, $200 \times 200 = 40\,000$

We use a small raised ^{2} to mean squared.

Example 3^2 means **3 squared**, or 3×3, which equals **9**; $5^2 = 5 \times 5 = 25$ and $10^2 = 10 \times 10 = 100$

Did you know?

Square numbers are called square because they can be drawn as squares.

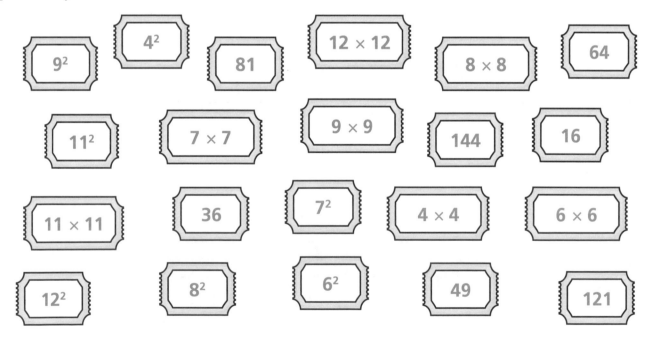

| 1 | 4 | 9 | 16 | 25 | 36 | 49 |

Activities

1 Join any tickets that show the same amount.

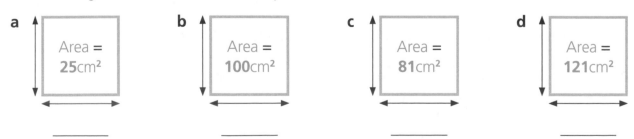

9²   4²   81   12 × 12   8 × 8   64

11²   7 × 7   9 × 9   144   16

11 × 11   36   7²   4 × 4   6 × 6

12²   8²   6²   49   121

2 Find the lengths of the sides of these squares.

a
Area =
25cm²

b
Area =
100cm²

c
Area =
81cm²

d
Area =
121cm²

_____   _____   _____   _____

Roman numerals to 100

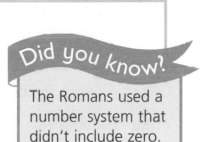
Activities

1 Work out the value of each of these.

a VIII _____

b XIV _____

c XXIII _____

d XXXVII _____

e XLIII _____

f LXI _____

g LXXXIII _____

h XCIV _____

2 Write each of these in Roman numerals.

a 16 _____

b 27 _____

c 41 _____

d 52 _____

e 39 _____

f 67 _____

g 86 _____

h 99 _____

3 True or false?

a XII + V = XVII _____

b XL + X = LX _____

c XXIX + I = XXX _____

d C   I = XCIX _____

e XLIX + LI = C _____

f X + LXXXIX = C _____

Roman numerals to 1000

Activities

1 Work out the value of each of these.

a CDLX _____

b CDLXIX _____

c DCLXV _____

d DCCIX _____

e DV _____

f DIX _____

g CM _____

h CMXI _____

2 Write each of these in Roman numerals.

a 176 _____

b 587 _____

c 401 _____

d 524 _____

e 396 _____

f 687 _____

g 876 _____

h 939 _____

3 True or false?

a D + V = DV _____

b M − X = MX _____

c CD + V = CDV _____

d CDIX − I = CDVIII _____

e M − DI = CDXCIX _____

f C + CCC = CD _____

Number Patterns & Algebra

Cube numbers

Some numbers are known as cube numbers, such as **1**, **8**, **27** and **64**. Cube numbers are the result of multiplying three of the same number together.

Example $1 \times 1 \times 1 = 1$, $2 \times 2 \times 2 = 8$, $3 \times 3 \times 3 = 27$, $4 \times 4 \times 4 = 64$, $5 \times 5 \times 5 = 125$...

We use a small raised ³ to mean cubed.

Example 3^3 means **3 cubed** or **3 × 3 × 3**, which equals **27**

Cube numbers are called this as cubes can be made from this number of small cubes.

Activities

1 Join any tickets that show the same amount.

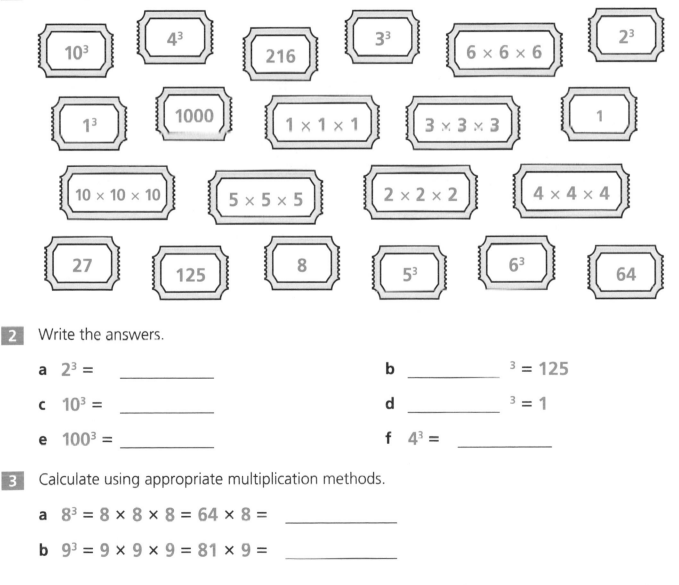

2 Write the answers.

a $2^3 =$ _____

b _____ $^3 = 125$

c $10^3 =$ _____

d _____ $^3 = 1$

e $100^3 =$ _____

f $4^3 =$ _____

3 Calculate using appropriate multiplication methods.

a $8^3 = 8 \times 8 \times 8 = 64 \times 8 =$ _____

b $9^3 = 9 \times 9 \times 9 = 81 \times 9 =$ _____

Finding factors 1

Explanation

A **factor** is a whole number that divides **exactly** into another number.

The factors of **12** are **1**, **2**, **3**, **4**, **6** and **12**, because each of these numbers divides exactly into **12**.

Look for factors by finding pairs of numbers that multiply to make your number.

Example Find the factors of 12.   **1 × 12, 2 × 6, 3 × 4**

Activities

1   Write the lengths of the sides of these rectangles. Use your answers to write all the factors of **24**.

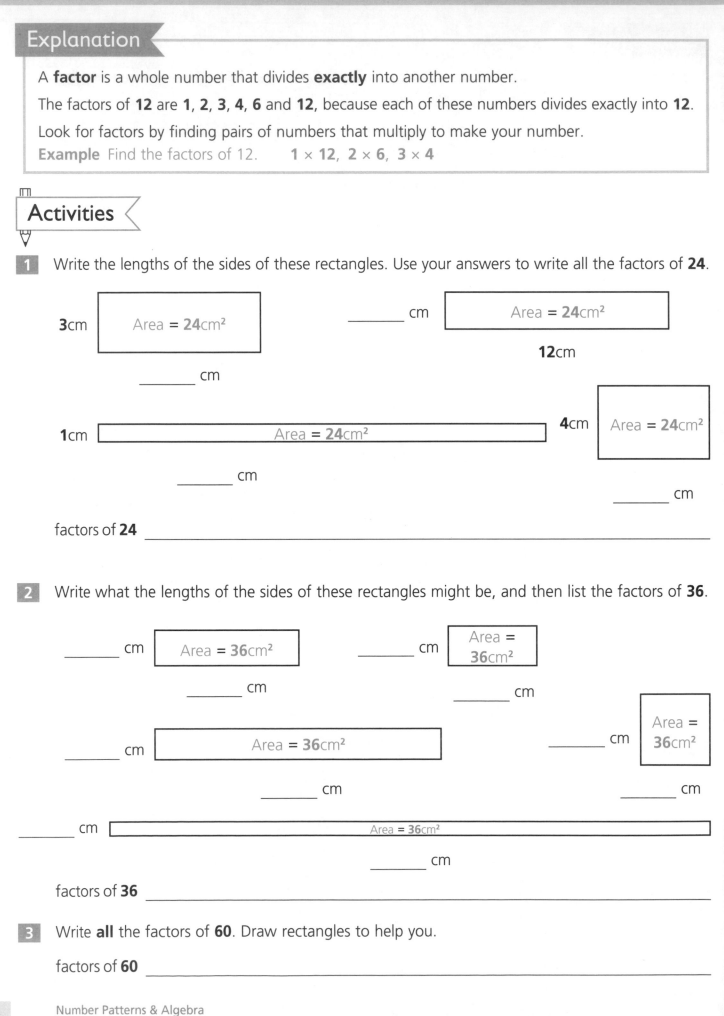

3cm   Area = **24**cm²

_____ cm   Area = **24**cm²

_____ cm

12cm

_____ cm

1cm   Area = **24**cm²

4cm   Area = **24**cm²

_____ cm

_____ cm

factors of **24** _____

2   Write what the lengths of the sides of these rectangles might be, and then list the factors of **36**.

_____ cm   Area = **36**cm²

_____ cm   Area = **36**cm²

_____ cm

_____ cm

_____ cm   Area = **36**cm²

_____ cm   Area = **36**cm²

_____ cm

_____ cm

_____ cm   Area = **36**cm²

_____ cm

factors of **36** _____

3   Write **all** the factors of **60**. Draw rectangles to help you.

factors of **60** _____

Number Patterns & Algebra

Finding factors 2

Explanation

You can use this method to make sure that you have found all the factors of a number.

Example Find all the factors of **48**.

Start with **1** and its partner that multiplies to **48**.	**1**	**48**		
Now try **2**	**2**	**24**		
Try **3**	**3**	**16**		
Try **4**	**4**	**12**		
Try **5**	**5̸**		**5** is not a factor of **48**	
Try **6**	**6**	**8**		
Try **7**	**7̸**		**7** is not a factor of **48**	
Try **8**	**8**			

We already know **8** is a factor, so when we have 'turned the corner' we know we have found all the factors.

So, the factors of **48** are **1**, **2**, **3**, **4**, **6**, **8**, **12**, **16**, **24** and **48**.

Activities

1 Find all the factors of:

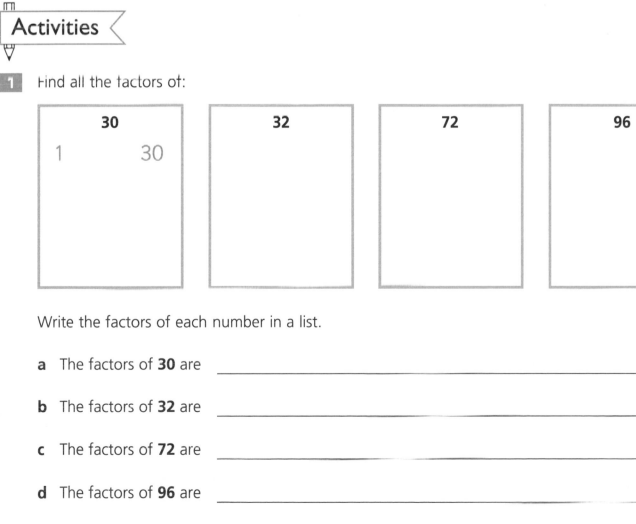

30	32	72	96
1 30			

Write the factors of each number in a list.

a The factors of **30** are _____

b The factors of **32** are _____

c The factors of **72** are _____

d The factors of **96** are _____

Progress test 3

1 Write the first **10** square numbers.

___1___ ___4___ _____ _____ _____ _____ _____ _____ _____ _____

2 Answer these questions.

a $7^2 =$

b $8^2 =$

c $9^2 =$

3 Write each of these in Roman numerals.

a 8 _____

b 14 _____

c 45 _____

d 570 _____

e 147 _____

f 900 _____

4 Work out the value of these numbers written in Roman numerals.

a LX _____

b XXIV _____

c LXIX _____

d XC _____

e DC _____

f DIV _____

g CMI _____

h CDXCIII _____

5 Answer these questions.

a $2^3 =$ _____

b $5^3 =$ _____

c $10^3 =$ _____

6 Find all the factors of the numbers below and write them in a list.

a 36 _____

b 48 _____

c 100 _____

Number Patterns & Algebra

Common factors

Explanation

Sometimes two or more numbers have a factor in common. These factors are called **common factors**.

The numbers **36** and **45** both have the factor **9**, so **9** is a common factor of **36** and **45**. Pairs or sets of numbers can have one or many common factors, for example, **16** and **24** have the common factors **2**, **4** and **8**.

The factor **1** doesn't count, as all whole numbers share this.

Activities

1 Find the common factor of each pair of numbers.

    a **28** and **21** have the common factor _____

    b **15** and **9** have the common factor _____

    c **14** and **20** have the common factor _____

    d **88** and **55** have the common factor _____

2 Find the common factors of each pair of numbers.

    a **12** and **16** _____ and _____

    b **30** and **40** _____, _____ and _____

    c **24** and **36** _____, _____, _____, _____ and _____

3 Write all the common factors of each set of numbers.

    a **6, 18** and **30** _____

    b **21, 42** and **49** _____

    c **15, 30** and **45** _____

    d **12, 24** and **48** _____

Recognising prime numbers 1

Explanation

Prime numbers are numbers that only have **two** factors, the number itself and **1**.
These numbers are all prime numbers.

	Factors			Factors
2	**1** and **2**		13	**1** and **13**
3	**1** and **3**		29	**1** and **29**
11	**1** and **11**		43	**1** and **43**

Note that **1** isn't a prime number because it only has one factor.

Activities

1 Follow each instruction and colour the squares you land on. **Don't** colour the squares you start on.

a Start on **2**.
    Count in twos.

b Start on **3**.
    Count in threes.

c Start on **4**.
    Count in fours.

d Start on **5**.
    Count in fives.

e Start on **6**.
    Count in sixes.

f Start on **7**.
    Count in sevens.

g Start on **8**.
    Count in eights.

h Start on **9**.
    Count in nines.

i Start on **10**.
    Count in tens.

1	2	3	4	5	6	7	8	9	10
11	12	13	14	15	16	17	18	19	20
21	22	23	24	25	26	27	28	29	30
31	32	33	34	35	36	37	38	39	40
41	42	43	44	45	46	47	48	49	50
51	52	53	54	55	56	57	58	59	60
61	62	63	64	65	66	67	68	69	70
71	72	73	74	75	76	77	78	79	80
81	82	83	84	85	86	87	88	89	90
91	92	93	94	95	96	97	98	99	100

You should have **25** numbers that are **not** coloured. Write them here.

_____

_____

These are the **25** prime numbers that lie between **1** and **100**.

Recognising prime numbers 2

Explanation

It is important to be able to recognise prime numbers and be able to say whether any number up to **100** is prime or non-prime. Non-prime numbers are sometimes called composite numbers.

- Remember that the only even prime number is **2**, so if a number is even it isn't prime.
- Two-digit numbers ending in **5** are not prime as they can be divided by **5**.
- Primes usually end in **1**, **3**, **7** and **9**, but not every number ending in **1**, **3**, **7** or **9** is a prime number.

Activities

1   Shade all the prime numbers.

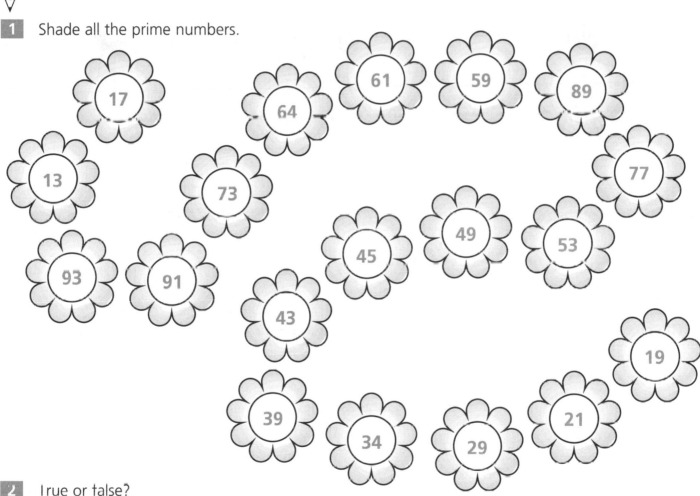

2   True or false?

a   **51** is not prime as it is has the factors **3** and **17**.   _____

b   **41** is not prime as it has the factors **4** and **11**.   _____

c   If you add **1** to a prime number other than **2**, you will always get an even number.   _____

d   If you choose a square number up to **100** and subtract **1** from it you will get a prime number.   _____

Factorising numbers into prime factors

Explanation

On pages 26 and 27 you learnt how to find **factors**, and on pages 30 and 31 you found out about **prime numbers**. Both these ideas can be used together to find **prime factors**.

Activities

1 Write pairs of factors of the number on the trees. Write them on the leaves.

a   b   c

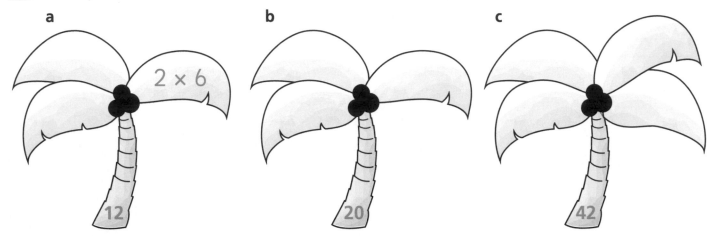

2 For each of the numbers in the trees above, write down any factors that are prime numbers.

     a   12   2, _____   b   20 _____   c   42 _____

The prime factors of **12** are **2**, **2** and **3** because **2 × 2 × 3 = 12** and **2** and **3** are prime numbers.

In the same way, the prime factors of **20** are **2**, **2** and **5** because **2 × 2 × 5 = 20** and **2** and **5** are prime numbers.

The prime factors of **42** are **2**, **3** and **7** because **2 × 3 × 7 = 42**.

When writing prime factors, you:

- use prime numbers only
- sometimes use the same prime number more than once.

---

3 Write the prime factors of these numbers as multiplication questions.

     a   8   ___ 2 × 2 × 2 ___   b   16 _____   c   24 _____

     d   32 _____   e   36 _____   f   40 _____

     g   60 _____   h   27 _____   i   96 _____

Finding common multiples

Explanation

On page 8, you learnt that a **multiple** is a number that is in a times table.

Multiples of **4** are **4, 8, 12, 16, 20, 24, 28, 32, 36, 40, 44,** ... and they carry on in fours.
Multiples of **10** go up in tens and include **50, 60, 230** and **1690**.

Numbers often have some of the same multiples as other numbers:

Example Multiples of **3**: 3   6   9   (12)   15   18   21   (24) ...

 Multiples of **4**: 4   8   (12)   16   20   (24) ...

12 and **24** are **common multiples** of **3** and **4**, because **3** and **4** have those multiples in common.

Activities

1   Write the first 10 multiples of **3** and **5**. Draw a ring around any common multiples.

3 _____

5 _____

2   Write the first 10 multiples of **4** and **6**. Draw a ring around any common multiples.

4 _____

6 _____

Look at the common multiples of **3** and **5** above. The **smallest (or lowest) common multiple**
of **3** and **5** is **15** because **15** is the smallest (or lowest) number that is a multiple of both **3** and **5**.
The smallest (or lowest) common multiple of **4** and **6** is **12**.

3   Write the smallest common multiple of:

a **3** and **4** _____

b **3** and **6** _____

c **8** and **12** _____

d **6** and **9** _____

e **7** and **6** _____

f **2, 3** and **6** _____

Progress test 4

1 Write all the common factors for each pair of numbers.

    a **24** and **30** _____

    b **27** and **45** _____

2 Write all the common factors of each set of numbers.

    a **14**, **42** and **56** _____

    b **12**, **24** and **40** _____

3 Write six prime numbers.

_____

4 Tick or cross to show whether each number is prime or not.

56   19   8   9   27   2   23   33   29   71

5 Write the prime factors of these numbers as multiplication questions.

    a 30 _____   **b** 28 _____   **c** 72 _____

6 Answer these questions.

    a Write four common multiples of **3** and **5**. _____

    b Write four common multiples of **6** and **4**. _____

    c Write four common multiples of **2** and **7**. _____

7 Write the smallest common multiple of:

    a **2** and **8** _____   **b** **4** and **9** _____   **c** **2**, **3** and **8** _____

Explaining a formula in words

These questions are all similar. They can all be solved in a similar way.

How many days are there in 6 weeks?	How many days are there in 31 weeks?	How many days are there in 324 weeks?

6 × 7 = **42** days   31 × 7 = **217** days   324 × 7 = **2268** days

Each question can be solved by **multiplying the number of weeks by 7**, because there are **7** days in a week.

Activities

1 These questions are all similar. Explain in words how you could solve them.

a

How many hours are there in **5** days?   How many hours are there in **25** days?   How many hours are there in **105** days?

_____

_____

b

How many months are there in **9** years?   How many months are there in **25** years?   How many months are there in **150** years?

_____

_____

c

How much change will I get from **£50** if I buy **3** DVDs costing **£6** each?   How much change will I get from **£50** if I buy **5** DVDs costing **£6** each?   How much change will I get from **£50** if I buy **7** DVDs costing **£6** each?

_____

_____

Explaining a formula using letters and symbols

These questions are all similar. They can all be solved in a similar way.

| How many days are there in 8 weeks? | How many days are there in 27 weeks? | How many days are there in 371 weeks? |

A **formula** can be used to answer any question of this type.

A formula is a quick way of writing a mathematical rule.

Example number of days = **7 × n**   or   number of days = **7n**

'**n**' is a code that stands for the number of weeks.

To answer the questions, swap **n** for the number of weeks given. This is called **substituting**.

| Number of days in 8 weeks | = **7 × n**
= **7 × 8**
= 56 | Number of days in 27 weeks | = **7 × n**
= **7 × 27**
= 189 | Number of days in 371 weeks | = **7 × n**
= **7 × 371**
= 2597 |

Activities

1 These questions are all similar. Write a formula to show how you could solve them.

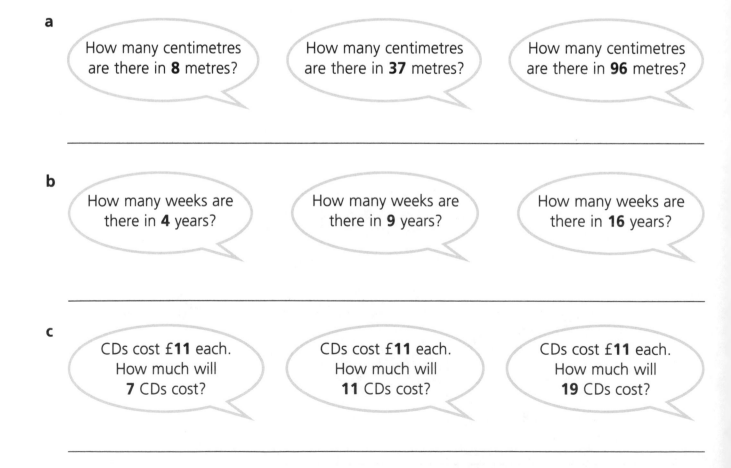

a

| How many centimetres are there in **8** metres? | How many centimetres are there in **37** metres? | How many centimetres are there in **96** metres? |

_____

b

| How many weeks are there in **4** years? | How many weeks are there in **9** years? | How many weeks are there in **16** years? |

_____

c

| CDs cost £**11** each. How much will **7** CDs cost? | CDs cost £**11** each. How much will **11** CDs cost? | CDs cost £**11** each. How much will **19** CDs cost? |

_____

Simple algebra

Explanation

Algebra is a part of maths where **letters** are used to represent **numbers**.

These **symbols** are used in place of numbers. Can you work out what each stands for?

▲ + 3 = 7   20 − ⬤ = 8   ■ × 3 = 12   24 ÷ ◆ = 4

Did you know?

An Arabic mathematician called Al-Khuwarizmi first used the word algebra over 1000 years ago.

Algebra uses **letters** in place of numbers in the same way.

Example $a + 4 = 9$ $23 − b = 16$ $c × 5 = 20$

a stands for a number. When you add 4 to *a* you get 9. So *a* must be 5.	*b* stands for a number. When you take *b* from 23 you get 16. So *b* must stand for 7.	*c* stands for a number. When you multiply *c* by 5 you get 20. So *c* must stand for 4.

Activities

1 Join each situation to its formula.

a
Jake has **c** pence. He spends **4** pence. How much does he have now?

$\frac{1}{2}c$

b
Isha has **9** pence. She finds **c** pence. How much does she have now?

$c + 4$

c
Jess eats **c** bags of crisps. Alice eats twice as many. How many does Alice eat?

$8 + c$

d
Ruby spends £**c** in the clothes shop and £**4** in the CD shop. How much does she spend?

$9 + c$

e
Oliver scores **c** goals. Toby scores half as many. How many goals does Toby score?

$c − 4$

f
Henry earns £**8** in the morning and £**c** in the afternoon. How much does he earn in total?

$2c$

Term-to-term rule

On page 14, you practised explaining a sequence in words, by giving the difference between adjacent numbers in the sequence. These numbers are known as terms. The 'term-to-term' rule tells you how to generate a sequence.

Example 7,   9,   11,   13,   15,   17 ...   The term-to-term rule for this sequence is:
Start at 7. Each term increases by 2.

Example 52,   47,   42,   37,   32   ...   The term-to-term rule for this sequence is:
Start at 52. Each term decreases by 5.

Activities

1 Write the term-to-term rule for each sequence.

a 9,   12,   15,   18,   21,   ...

Start at _____ . Each term _____

b 93,   88,   83,   78,   73,   ...

Start at _____ . Each term _____

c 5,   9,   13,   17,   21,   25,   ...

Start at _____ . Each term _____

d 100,   89,   78,   67,   56,   45,   ...

Start at _____ . Each term _____

2 Write the first 10 terms of the sequence with the term-to-term rule given.

a Start at **17**. Each term increases by **5**.

_____ _____ _____ _____ _____ _____ _____ _____ _____ _____

b Start at **100**. Each term decreases by **9**.

_____ _____ _____ _____ _____ _____ _____ _____ _____ _____

c Start at **–5**. Each term increases by **11**.

_____ _____ _____ _____ _____ _____ _____ _____ _____ _____

d Start at **–17**. Each term decreases by **5**.

_____ _____ _____ _____ _____ _____ _____ _____ _____ _____

Using algebra to describe sequences

Explanation

There is another way to describe sequences other than the term-to-term rule. Algebra can be used to describe how a sequence can be generated.

Example Look at this sequence. **3, 6, 9, 12, 15, 18, 21, 24, 27 ...**

The term-to-term rule of this sequence is: **Start at 3. Each term increases by 3.**

But the sequence can also be described as **3n** where **n** stands for the position of the term. This means that:

* the first term (where **n** is **1**) will be $3 \times 1 = 3$
* the second term (where **n** is **2**) will be $3 \times 2 = 6$
* the third term (where **n** is **3**) will be $3 \times 3 = 9$ and so on.

Activities

1 Fill in the table to write the first 10 terms of the sequence **5n**.

n =	1	2	3	4	5	6	7	8	9	10
5n =	5	10								

2 Fill in the table to write the first 10 terms of the sequence **8n**.

n =	1	2	3	4	5	6	7	8	9	10
8n =										

3 Fill in the table to write the first 10 terms of the sequence **2n + 1**.

n =	1	2	3	4	5	6	7	8	9	10
2n + 1 =	3	5	7							

4 Fill in the table to write the first 10 terms of the sequence **5n − 1**.

n =	1	2	3	4	5	6	7	8	9	10
5n − 1 =	4	9	14							

5 Fill in the table to write the first 10 terms of the sequence **3n + 12**.

n =	1	2	3	4	5	6	7	8	9	10
3n + 12 =	15	18	21							

Unknowns and variables

Activities

1   Write all the possibilities if *a* + *b* = 6,
       where *a* and *b* are integers from **1** to **5**.

> If *a* is _____, *b* is _____
>
> If *a* is _____, *b* is _____
>
> If *a* is _____, *b* is _____
>
> If *a* is _____, *b* is _____
>
> If *a* is _____, *b* is _____

2   Write all the possibilities if *a* − *b* = 2,
       where *a* and *b* are integers from **1** to **5**.

> If *a* is _____, *b* is _____
>
> If *a* is _____, *b* is _____
>
> If *a* is _____, *b* is _____

3   List all the possibilities if *a* − *b* = 1,
       where *a* and *b* are integers from **1** to **5**.

4   *m* + *n* = 7, where *m* and *n* are integers from **0** to **7**. List all the possible values for *m* and *n*.

Final test

1 Count back in tens starting from:

176 ____ ____ ____ ____ ____ ____ ____ ____ ____

2 Count back in hundreds starting from:

2435 _____ _____ _____ _____ _____ _____ _____ _____

3 Draw a ring around any **odd** numbers you can see in this list.

26   53   162   535   1041   2309

4 Count back in fives starting from:

72 ____ ____ ____ ____ ____ ____ ____ ____ ____

5 Fill in the missing numbers in these sequences.

a 36, 33, ____, 27, 24, ____, 18, 15, ____, 9, 6, 3 …

b 56, 48, 40, ____, 24, ____, 8, ____ …

c 44, ____, 36, ____, 28, ____, 20, 16, ____, 8 …

6 Circle all the multiples of **25**. Cross the multiples of **50**.

250   127   512   502   525   200   575

7 Count on in steps of **250** to continue the sequence.

1500 _____ _____ _____ _____ _____ _____ _____

8 Count on to continue these sequences:

a in sixes   0, 6, ____ ____ ____ ____ ____ ____ ____ ____ ____

b in sevens 0, 7, ____ ____ ____ ____ ____ ____ ____ ____ ____

c in nines   0, 9, ____ ____ ____ ____ ____ ____ ____ ____ ____

9 Circle all the multiples of **8**.

44   60   88   96   16   54   72   56   32   48   18   24

10 Fill in the missing numbers in these sequences.

a ☐—☐—102—☐—☐—☐—26—☐

b ☐—15—☐—☐—36—☐—☐—☐

11 Continue each sequence and then explain it.

a 7 — $7\frac{1}{3}$ — $7\frac{2}{3}$ — ☐ — ☐ — ☐   _____
                                                      _____
                                                      _____

b $3\frac{3}{4}$ — 4 — $4\frac{1}{4}$ — ☐ — ☐ — ☐   _____
                                                      _____
                                                      _____

12 Fill in the missing fractions or mixed numbers.

a $\frac{2}{100}$, $\frac{3}{100}$, $\frac{4}{100}$, ☐, ☐, ☐, ☐, ☐, $\frac{10}{100}$, $\frac{11}{100}$, ☐, ☐ ...

b $\frac{8}{10}$, $\frac{9}{10}$, 1, $1\frac{1}{10}$, $1\frac{2}{10}$, ☐, ☐, $1\frac{5}{10}$, ☐, ☐, ☐, ☐, ☐ ...

13 Continue these sequences.

a 6, 4, 2, 0, −2, −4, ____ ____ ____ ____ ____ ____

b 33, 28, 23, 18, 13, ____ ____ ____ ____ ____ ____

c −67, −56, −45, −34, −23, ____ ____ ____ ____ ____ ____

14 Work out the value of each of these.

    a XXVII   _____   **b** XCV   _____

    c DCCIV   _____   **d** CMXII   _____

15 Write each of these in Roman numerals.

    a 18   _____   **b** 29   _____

    c 174   _____   **d** 392   _____

16 Write the answers.

    a $2^2 =$ _____   **b** $2^3 =$ _____

    c _____$^2 = 64$ **d** _____$^3 - 64$

    e _____$^3 = 1$ **f** $10^3 =$ _____

17 Write the factors of **48**. _____

18 Find the common factors of each set of numbers.

    a **32** and **28**   _____

    b **28**, **42** and **56**   _____

19 Tick or cross to show whether each number is prime or not.

    54   15   13   9   27   2   17   33   29   19

20 These questions are all similar. Explain in words how you could solve them.

    How many hours are there in **15** days?

    How many hours are there in **29** days?

    How many hours are there in **179** days?

_____

_____

21 These questions are all similar. Write a formula to show how you could solve them.

If cinema tickets cost £**4** ...

... how much do **6** cinema tickets cost?	... how much do **17** cinema tickets cost?	... how much do **93** cinema tickets cost?

_____

22 Write a formula to match each situation.

a Nisha has **y** sweets. She gives **1** away. How many has she now?   _____

b Jamie is **b** years old. His brother Max is twice as old. How old is Max?   _____

c A coat costing £**25** is reduced by £**d** in the sale. How much does it cost now?   _____

23 Write the term-to-term rule for this sequence.

8,   11,   14,   17,   20 ...

Start at _____ . Each term _____

24 Fill in the table to write the first 10 terms of the sequence **2n − 1**.

$n =$	1	2	3	4	5	6	7	8	9	10
$2n - 1 =$	1	3								

25 List all the possibilities if **a + b = 4**, where **a** and **b** are integers from **0** to **5**.

Answers to Activities

Page 4: Odd and even numbers

1 56, 78, 814

2 99, 175, 681

3 a even numbers either side of an odd number
   b correct addition of three odd numbers
   c correct subtraction
   d correct multiplication

Page 5: Counting on from zero in steps of 2, 5, 3, 4 and 8

1 a 4, 6, 8, 10, 12, 14, 16, 18, 20, 22
   b 10, 15, 20, 25, 30, 35, 40, 45, 50, 55
   c 6, 9, 12, 15, 18, 21, 24, 27, 30, 33
   d 8, 12, 16, 20, 24, 28, 32, 36, 40, 44
   e 16, 24, 32, 40, 48, 56, 64, 72, 80, 88

2 a All even and the numbers in the fours sequence are double those in the twos sequence.
   b All even and the numbers in the eights sequence are double those in the fours sequence.

3 a 32, 16, 0
   b 27, 21, 12
   c 44, 36, 28, 12

Page 6: Counting on and back in tens

1 a 70, 80, 90, 100, 110, 120, 130, 140, 150, 160, 170
   b 103, 113, 123, 133, 143, 153, 163, 173, 183, 193, 203

2 a 142, 132, 122, 112, 102, 92, 82, 72, 62, 52, 42
   b 208, 198, 188, 178, 168, 158, 148, 138, 128, 118, 108

3 a 37, 47, 57, 67, 77, 87, 97, 107, 117, 127
   b 73, 83, 93, 103, 113, 123, 133, 143, 153, 163
   c 205, 195, 185, 175, 165, 155, 145, 135, 125, 115
   d 388, 378, 368, 358, 348, 338, 328, 318, 308, 298
   e 6216, 6226, 6236, 6246, 6256, 6266, 6276, 6286, 6296, 6306
   f 1174, 1184, 1194, 1204, 1214, 1224, 1234, 1244, 1254, 1264

Page 7: Counting on and back in hundreds

1 a 400, 500, 600, 700, 800, 900, 1000, 1100, 1200
   b 953, 1053, 1153, 1253, 1353, 1453, 1553, 1653, 1753
   c 1642, 1742, 1842, 1942, 2042, 2142, 2242, 2342, 2442

2 a 1300, 1200, 1100, 1000, 900, 800, 700, 600, 500
   b 3682, 3582, 3482, 3382, 3282, 3182, 3082, 2982, 2882
   c 7761, 7661, 7561, 7461, 7361, 7261, 7161, 7061, 6961

3 a 1000, 1100, 1200, 1300, 1400, 1500, 1600, 1700, 1800, 1900
   b 6217, 6317, 6417, 6517, 6617, 6717, 6817, 6917, 7017, 7117
   c 5442, 5342, 5242, 5142, 5042, 4942, 4842, 4742, 4642, 4542
   d 7851, 7751, 7651, 7551, 7451, 7351, 7251, 7151, 7051, 6951
   e 8436, 8536, 8636, 8736, 8836, 8936, 9036, 9136, 9236, 9336

Page 8: Recognising multiples of 2, 3, 4, 5 and 10

1 a any five even numbers
   b any five multiples of 3
   c any five multiples of 5
   d any five multiples of 8
   e any five multiples of 50
   f any five multiples of 100

2 a 44, 12, 6, 60, 100, 38, 94
   b 9, 42, 18, 12, 15, 27, 63, 39
   c 44, 12, 60, 100
   d 25, 15, 40

3

Page 9: Counting in multiples of 25, 50, 100, 250 and 1000

1 a 500, 550, 600, 650, 700, 750, 800
b 1300, 1350, 1400, 1450, 1500, 1550, 1600
c 8850, 8900, 8950, 9000, 9050, 9100, 9150

2 a 350, 375, 400, 425, 450, 475, 500
b 3575, 3600, 3625, 3650, 3675, 3700, 3725
c 7900, 7925, 7950, 7975, 8000, 8025, 8050

3 a 6100, 6125, 6150, 6175, 6200, 6225, 6250
b 5000, 5500, 6000, 6500, 7000, 7500, 8000
c Add 50: 7500, 7550, 7600, 7650, 7700, 7750, 7800
d Add 1000: 7000, 8000, 9000, 10000, 11000, 12000, 13000
e Add 250: 7500, 7750, 8000, 8250, 8500, 8750, 9000
Circle 7500, 8000, 9000.

Page 11: Counting on from zero in steps of 6, 7 and 9

1 a 12, 18, 24, 30, 36, 42, 48, 54, 60, 66, 72
b 14, 21, 28, 35, 42, 49, 56, 63, 70, 77, 84
c 18, 27, 36, 45, 54, 63, 72, 81, 90, 99, 108

2 all even

3 a 42 b 63 c 18, 36, 54, 72

4 a The numbers in the sixes sequence are double those in the threes sequence.
b The numbers in the nines sequence are three times those in the threes sequence.

5 a 63, 49, 35, 28
b 42, 54, 66, 72
c 81, 63, 36
d 66, 60, 48, 36

Page 12: Recognising multiples of 6, 7, 8 and 9

1 a any five multiples of 6
b any five multiples of 7
c any five multiples of 8
d any five multiples of 9

2 a 18, 48, 60, 6, 90, 84
b 35, 42, 63, 56, 70, 105
c 40, 72, 16, 24, 88
d 27, 90, 54, 72, 45, 99, 63, 36

3

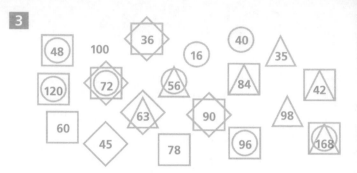

Page 13: Finding missing numbers in sequences

1 a 13, 17, 21, 25
b 17, 22, 27, 32
c 23, 29, 35, 41
d 26, 33, 40, 47
e 143, 132, 121, 110
f 195, 183, 171, 159

2 a 37, 41, 45, 49, 53, 57, 61, 65
b 80, 73, 66, 59, 52, 45, 38, 31
c 38, 59, 80, 101, 122, 143, 164, 185

Page 14: Explaining number sequences

1 a 15, 8, 1. The decreasing sequence starts with 36. The difference is 7 each time.
b 38, 23, 8. The decreasing sequence starts with 83. The difference is 15 each time.
c 15, 21. The increasing sequence starts with 1. The difference increases by one each time, e.g. 2, 3, 4, 5 …
d 63, 75, 87. The increasing sequence starts with 27. The difference is 12 each time.
e 40, 8. The decreasing sequence starts with 70. The difference is doubled each time, starting with 2, e.g. 2, 4, 8 …

Page 15: Fraction sequences

1 a $4\frac{1}{2}$, 5, $5\frac{1}{2}$, 6, $6\frac{1}{2}$, 7
b $10\frac{1}{2}$, 10, $9\frac{1}{2}$, 9, $8\frac{1}{2}$, 8

2 a $5\frac{1}{2}$, $5\frac{3}{4}$, 6, $6\frac{1}{4}$, $6\frac{1}{2}$, $6\frac{3}{4}$
b $18\frac{1}{4}$, 18, $17\frac{3}{4}$, $17\frac{1}{2}$, $17\frac{1}{4}$, 17

3 a $4\frac{1}{3}$, $4\frac{2}{3}$, 5, $5\frac{1}{3}$, $5\frac{2}{3}$, 6
b 15, $14\frac{2}{3}$, $14\frac{1}{3}$, 14, $13\frac{2}{3}$, $13\frac{1}{3}$

4 **a** 7, $6\frac{2}{3}$, $6\frac{1}{3}$. Starts at 8. Decreases by one-third each time.

b $5\frac{1}{2}$, $5\frac{3}{4}$, 6. Starts at $4\frac{3}{4}$. Increases by one-quarter each time.

c $19\frac{1}{2}$, 19, $18\frac{1}{2}$. Starts at 21. Decreases by one-half each time.

Page 16: Tenths and hundredths

1 **a** $\frac{5}{10}$, $\frac{6}{10}$, $\frac{8}{10}$, $\frac{13}{10}$, $\frac{14}{10}$ ($\frac{5}{10}$ and $\frac{10}{10}$ circled)

b $1\frac{3}{10}$, $1\frac{4}{10}$, $1\frac{6}{10}$, $1\frac{7}{10}$, $1\frac{8}{10}$, $1\frac{9}{10}$, 2 ($1\frac{5}{10}$ circled)

c 0.4, 0.6, 0.9, 1.3 (0.5 circled)

2 **a** $\frac{5}{100}$, $\frac{6}{100}$, $\frac{7}{100}$, $\frac{8}{100}$, $\frac{9}{100}$, $\frac{12}{100}$, $\frac{13}{100}$ ($\frac{10}{100}$ circled)

b $1\frac{2}{100}$, $1\frac{3}{100}$, $1\frac{5}{100}$, $1\frac{6}{100}$, $1\frac{7}{100}$, $1\frac{8}{100}$, $1\frac{9}{100}$

c 0.04, 0.09, 0.12

d 0.92, 0.97, 1 or 1.00

Page 17: Counting on and back with decimals

1 **a** 1.0, 1.1, 1.2, 1.3, 1.4, 1.5, 1.6

b 2.2, 2.4, 2.6, 2.8, 3.0, 3.2, 3.4

c 2.0, 2.25, 2.5, 2.75, 3.0, 3.25, 3.5

d 2.0, 2.5, 3.0, 3.5, 4.0, 4.5, 5.0

2 **a** 1 or 1.0, 0.9, 0.8. Starts at 1.3. Decreases by 0.1 (one-tenth) each time.

b 6.25, 6, 5.75. Starts at 7. Decreases by 0.25 (one-quarter) each time.

c 9.8, 10 or 10.0, 10.2. Starts at 9.2. Increases by 0.2 (one-fifth) each time.

Page 18: Counting on and back beyond zero

1 **a** 5, 4, 3, 2, 1, 0, –1

b 0, –1, –2, –3, –4, –5, –6

c –4, –5, –6, –7, –8, –9, –10

d –11, –12, –13, –14, –15, –16, –17

2 **a** 3, 4, 5, 6, 7, 8, 9

b 0, 1, 2, 3, 4, 5, 6

c –6, –5, –4, –3, –2, –1, 0

d –11, –10, –9, –8, –7, –6, –5

3 **a** 4, 3, 2, 1, 0, –1, –2, –3

b 0, –1, –2, –3, –4, –5, –6, –7

c 9, 10, –11, –12, –13, –14, –15, –16

Page 19: Negative numbers

1 **a** –2°C
b 7°C
c –7°C
d –4°C
e –14°C

2 **a** 8°C **b** 15°C
c 5°C **d** 15°C

3 **a** –5°C, –3°C, –1°C, 3°C, 5°C
b –10°C, –4°C, –1°C, 0°C, 8°C
c –3°C, –1.5°C, –1°C, 1.5°C, 2°C

4 **a** –6, 8, –10, –12, –14, –16
b 0, –5, –10, –15, –20, –25
c 6, 1, –4, –9, –14, –19
d –11, –1, 9, 19, 29, 39
e –8, –5, –2, 1, 4, 7

Page 20: Predicting numbers in a sequence

1 **a** yes **b** no **c** no **d** yes
e yes **f** yes **g** no **h** no
i no **j** yes **k** yes

Page 22: Square numbers

1 $4^2 = 4 \times 4 = 16$
$6^2 = 6 \times 6 = 36$
$7^2 = 7 \times 7 = 49$
$8^2 = 8 \times 8 = 64$
$9^2 = 9 \times 9 = 81$
$11^2 = 11 \times 11 = 121$
$12^2 = 12 \times 12 = 144$

2 **a** 5cm **b** 10cm **c** 9cm **d** 11cm

Page 23: Roman numerals to 100

1 **a** 8 **b** 14
c 23 **d** 37
e 43 **f** 61
g 83 **h** 94

2 **a** XVI **b** XXVII
c XLI **d** LII
e XXXIX **f** LXVII
g LXXXVI **h** XCIX

3 **a** true   **b** false
       c true   **d** true
       e true   **f** false

Page 24: Roman numerals to 1000

1 **a** 460   **b** 469
       c 665   **d** 709
       e 505   **f** 509
       g 900   **h** 911

2 **a** CLXXVI   **b** DLXXXVII
       c CDI   **d** DXXIV
       e CCCXCVI   **f** DCLXXXVII
       g DCCCLXXVI   **h** CMXXXIX

3 **a** true   **b** false
       c true   **d** true
       e true   **f** true

Page 25: Cube numbers

1 $1^3 = 1 \times 1 \times 1 = 1$
       $2^3 = 2 \times 2 \times 2 = 8$
       $3^3 = 3 \times 3 \times 3 = 27$
       $4^3 = 4 \times 4 \times 4 = 64$
       $5^3 = 5 \times 5 \times 5 = 125$
       $6^3 = 6 \times 6 \times 6 = 216$
       $10^3 = 10 \times 10 \times 10 = 1000$

2 **a** 8   **b** 5
       c 1000   **d** 1
       e 1 000 000 **f** 64

3 **a** 512
       b 729

Page 26: Finding factors 1

1 1, 2, 3, 4, 6, 8, 12, 24
2 1, 2, 3, 4, 6, 9, 12, 18, 36
3 1, 2, 3, 4, 5, 6, 10, 12, 15, 20, 30, 60

Page 27: Finding factors 2

1 **a** 1, 2, 3, 5, 6, 10, 15, 30
       b 1, 2, 4, 8, 16, 32
       c 1, 2, 3, 4, 6, 8, 9, 12, 18, 24, 36, 72
       d 1, 2, 3, 4, 6, 8, 12, 16, 24, 32, 48, 96

Page 29: Common factors

1 **a** 7   **b** 3   **c** 2   **d** 11
2 **a** 2, 4   **b** 2, 5, 10   **c** 2, 3, 4, 6, 12
3 **a** 2, 3, 6
       b 7
       c 3, 5, 15
       d 2, 3, 4, 6, 12

Page 30: Recognising prime numbers 1

1 2, 3, 5, 7, 11, 13, 17, 19, 23, 29, 31, 37, 41, 43, 47, 53, 59, 61, 67, 71, 73, 79, 83, 89, 97

Page 31: Recognising prime numbers 2

1 13, 17, 19, 29, 43, 53, 59, 61, 73, 89 shaded
2 **a** true   **b** false   **c** true   **d** false

Page 32: Factorising numbers into prime factors

1 **a** 1 × 12, 2 × 6, 3 × 4
       b 1 × 20, 2 × 10, 4 × 5
       c 1 × 42, 2 × 21, 7 × 6, 3 × 14
2 **a** 2, 3   **b** 2, 5   **c** 2, 3, 7
3 **a** 2 × 2 × 2   **b** 2 × 2 × 2 × 2
       c 2 × 2 × 2 × 3   **d** 2 × 2 × 2 × 2 × 2
       e 2 × 2 × 3 × 3   **f** 2 × 2 × 2 × 5
       g 2 × 2 × 3 × 5   **h** 3 × 3 × 3
       i 2 × 2 × 2 × 2 × 2 × 3

Page 33: Finding common multiples

1 common multiples: 15, 30
2 common multiples: 12, 24, 36
3 **a** 12   **b** 6   **c** 24
       d 18   **e** 42   **f** 6

Page 35: Explaining a formula in words

1 **a** Multiply the number of days by 24.
       b Multiply the number of years by 12.
       c Multiply £6 by the number of DVDs and subtract the answer from 50.

Page 36: Explaining a formula using letters and symbols

1 **a** number of centimetres = 100n
   b number of weeks = 52n
   c price in pounds = 11n

Page 37: Simple algebra

1 **a** $c - 4$ **b** $9 + c$ **c** $2c$
   d $c + 4$ **e** $\frac{1}{2}c$ **f** $8 + c$

Page 38: Term-to-term rule

1 **a** 9, increases by 3
   b 93, decreases by 5
   c 5, increases by 4
   d 100, decreases by 11

2 **a** 17, 22, 27, 32, 37, 42, 47, 52, 57, 62
   b 100, 91, 82, 73, 64, 55, 46, 37, 28, 19
   c −5, 6, 17, 28, 39, 50, 61, 72, 83, 94
   d −17, −22, −27, −32, −37, −42, −47, −52, −57, −62

Page 39: Using algebra to describe sequences

1 5, 10, 15, 20, 25, 30, 35, 40, 45, 50

2 8, 16, 24, 32, 40, 48, 56, 64, 72, 80

3 3, 5, 7, 9, 11, 13, 15, 17, 19, 21

4 4, 9, 14, 19, 24, 29, 34, 39, 44, 49

5 15, 18, 21, 24, 27, 30, 33, 36, 39, 42

Page 40: Unknowns and variables

1 $a = 1$, $b = 5$
   $a = 2$, $b = 4$
   $a = 3$, $b = 3$
   $a - 4$, $b = 2$
   $a = 5$, $b = 1$

2 $a = 5$, $b = 3$
   $a = 4$, $b = 2$
   $a = 3$, $b = 1$

3 $a = 5$, $b = 4$
   $a = 4$, $b = 3$
   $a = 3$, $b = 2$
   $a = 2$, $b = 1$

4 $m = 0$, $n = 7$
   $m = 1$, $n = 6$
   $m = 2$, $n = 5$
   $m = 3$, $n = 4$
   $m = 4$, $n = 3$
   $m = 5$, $n = 2$
   $m = 6$, $n = 1$
   $m = 7$, $n = 0$

Answers to Progress tests

PROGRESS TEST 1 – Page 10

1 3, 6, 9, 12, 15, 18, 21, 24, 27, 30, 33

2 8, 16, 24, 32, 40, 48, 56, 64, 72, 80, 88

3 88, 98, 108, 118, 128, 138, 148, 158, 168, 178, 188

4 166, 156, 146, 136, 126, 116, 106, 96, 86, 76

5 394, 494, 594, 694, 794, 894, 994, 1094, 1194

6 3572, 3472, 3372, 3272, 3172, 3072, 2972, 2872, 2772

7 34, 182, 780

8 **a** any five multiples of 3
   b any five multiples of 4

9
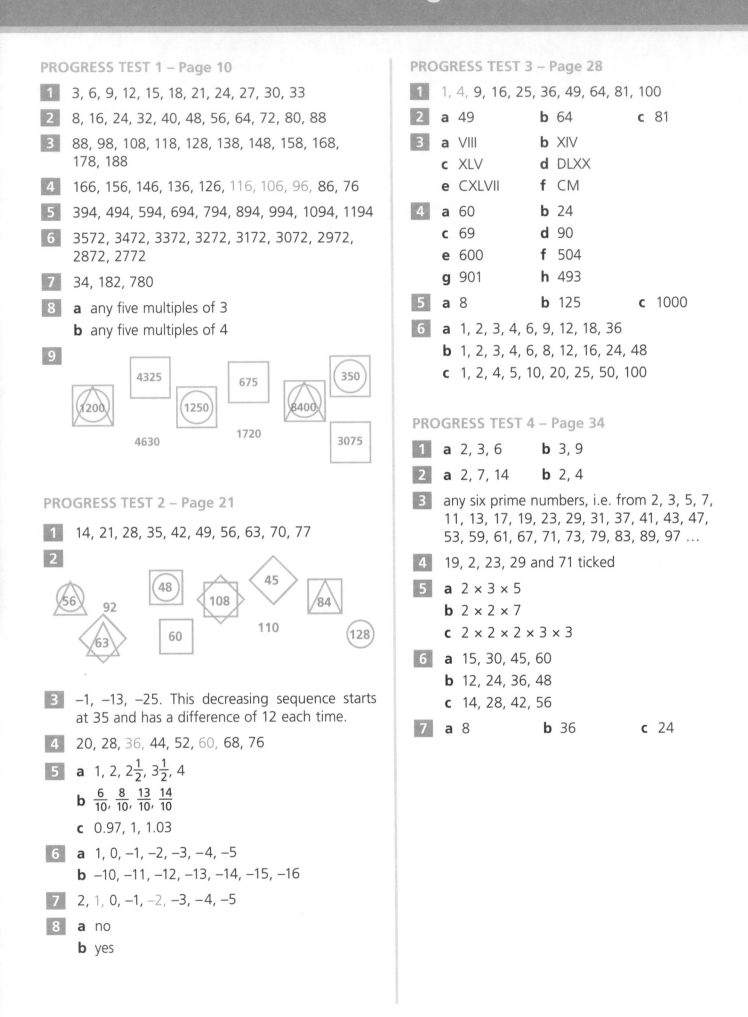

PROGRESS TEST 2 – Page 21

1 14, 21, 28, 35, 42, 49, 56, 63, 70, 77

2

3 −1, −13, −25. This decreasing sequence starts at 35 and has a difference of 12 each time.

4 20, 28, 36, 44, 52, 60, 68, 76

5 **a** 1, 2, $2\frac{1}{2}$, $3\frac{1}{2}$, 4
   b $\frac{6}{10}$, $\frac{8}{10}$, $\frac{13}{10}$, $\frac{14}{10}$
   c 0.97, 1, 1.03

6 **a** 1, 0, −1, −2, −3, −4, −5
   b −10, −11, −12, −13, −14, −15, −16

7 2, 1, 0, −1, −2, −3, −4, −5

8 **a** no
   b yes

PROGRESS TEST 3 – Page 28

1 1, 4, 9, 16, 25, 36, 49, 64, 81, 100

2 **a** 49   **b** 64   **c** 81

3 **a** VIII   **b** XIV
   c XLV   **d** DLXX
   e CXLVII   **f** CM

4 **a** 60   **b** 24
   c 69   **d** 90
   e 600   **f** 504
   g 901   **h** 493

5 **a** 8   **b** 125   **c** 1000

6 **a** 1, 2, 3, 4, 6, 9, 12, 18, 36
   b 1, 2, 3, 4, 6, 8, 12, 16, 24, 48
   c 1, 2, 4, 5, 10, 20, 25, 50, 100

PROGRESS TEST 4 – Page 34

1 **a** 2, 3, 6   **b** 3, 9

2 **a** 2, 7, 14   **b** 2, 4

3 any six prime numbers, i.e. from 2, 3, 5, 7, 11, 13, 17, 19, 23, 29, 31, 37, 41, 43, 47, 53, 59, 61, 67, 71, 73, 79, 83, 89, 97 …

4 19, 2, 23, 29 and 71 ticked

5 **a** 2 × 3 × 5
   b 2 × 2 × 7
   c 2 × 2 × 2 × 3 × 3

6 **a** 15, 30, 45, 60
   b 12, 24, 36, 48
   c 14, 28, 42, 56

7 **a** 8   **b** 36   **c** 24

Number Patterns & Algebra

Answers to Final test

FINAL TEST – Pages 41–44

1 166, 156, 146, 136, 126, 116, 106, 96, 86, 76

2 2335, 2235, 2135, 2035, 1935, 1835, 1735, 1635

3 53, 535, 1041, 2309

4 67, 62, 57, 52, 47, 42, 37, 32, 27, 22

5 a 30, 21, 12
  b 32, 16, 0
  c 40, 32, 24, 12

6 250, 525, 200 and 575 circled
  250 and 200 crossed

7 1750, 2000, 2250, 2500, 2750, 3000, 3250, 3500

8 a 12, 18, 24, 30, 36, 42, 48, 54, 60, 66
  b 14, 21, 28, 35, 42, 49, 56, 63, 70, 77
  c 18, 27, 36, 45, 54, 63, 72, 81, 90, 99

9 88, 96, 16, 72, 56, 32, 48 and 24 circled

10 a 140, 121, 102, 83, 64, 45, 26, 7
  b 8, 15, 22, 29, 36, 43, 50, 57

11 a 8, $8\frac{1}{3}$, $8\frac{2}{3}$. Start at 7. Count on in thirds.
  b $4\frac{1}{2}$, $4\frac{3}{4}$, 5. Start at $3\frac{3}{4}$. Count on in quarters.

12 a $\frac{5}{100}$, $\frac{6}{100}$, $\frac{7}{100}$, $\frac{8}{100}$, $\frac{9}{100}$, $\frac{12}{100}$, $\frac{13}{100}$
  b $1\frac{3}{10}$, $1\frac{4}{10}$, $1\frac{6}{10}$, $1\frac{7}{10}$, $1\frac{8}{10}$, $1\frac{9}{10}$, 2

13 a −6, −8, −10, −12, −14, −16
  b 8, 3, −2, −7, −12, −17
  c −12, −1, 10, 21, 32, 43

14 a 27   b 95
  c 704   d 912

15 a XVIII   b XXIX
  c CLXXIV   d CCCXCII

16 a 4   b 8
  c 8   d 4
  e 1   f 1000

17 1, 2, 3, 4, 6, 8, 12, 16, 24, 48

18 a 2 and 4
  b 2, 7 and 14

19 13, 2, 17, 29, 19 ticked

20 Multiply the number of days by 24.

21 cost = 4*n*

22 a *y* − 1
  b 2*b*
  c 25 − *d*

23 8, increases by 3

24 1, 3, 5, 7, 9, 11, 13, 15, 17, 19

25 *a* = 4, *b* = 0
  a = 3, *b* = 1
  a = 2, *b* = 2
  a = 1, *b* = 3
  a = 0, *b* = 4

Schofield & Sims I Understanding Maths

51